MY Fairy Tales
A STICKER STORYBOOK

Retold by Victoria Crenson
Illustrated by Thea Kliros

DERRYDALE BOOKS
New York / Avenel, New Jersey

How To Use Your Fairy Tale Sticker Storybook

In each story, some words have been left out. Find the correct stickers for those words from the sticker pages at the back of the book. Place the stickers in the correct spaces. The stickers are grouped by pages to help you. If you would like a hint, the missing words are listed in special boxes in each story.

Created and manufactured by arrangement with
Ottenheimer Publishers, Inc.
© 1993 Ottenheimer Publishers, Inc.
SF816C
All Rights Reserved.
This 1994 edition published by DERRYDALE BOOKS, distributed by
Outlet Book Company, Inc., a Random House Company,
40 Engelhard Avenue, Avenel, New Jersey 07001
Printed in Hong Kong.

ISBN: 0-517-10308-7

8 7 6 5 4 3 2 1

TABLE OF CONTENTS

JACK
AND THE
BEANSTALK

Long ago there lived a widow and her son, Jack.

One day the poor woman said to Jack,

"We cannot afford to buy even

a bit of  . There is no choice

but to sell our cow."

Jack offered to take the to

market and sell her.

On the way to the village,

he met a funny-looking

man coming down

the .

"I'll make you a trade for that skinny cow," said the  . "Here, take this handful of magic  ."

Jack was happy to make the swap. He ran all the way home to show his mother what a clever deal he had made for the cow.

Jack's  was angry. "How could you be so foolish? There are no such things as magic beans."

MY STICKER WORDS
bread
cow
road
man
beans
mother

She took the beans and threw them

out the window into the  . "Now

go to bed, for there is no supper."

The next morning Jack and his

mother had a big surprise! During the

night, the beans had sprouted. They

had grown into a thick beanstalk so tall

that it was lost in the  .

"I wonder where it ends?" said Jack.

-6-

MY STICKER
WORDS
garden
clouds
beanstalk
sky
boys

He jumped on the _____ and began climbing.

He climbed and climbed all day until he reached

the _____ . At the very top, he found a path that took him

to the front door of an enormous house. When Jack knocked,

a tall woman opened the door.

"Please, ma'am, I'm hungry and thirsty," begged Jack.

"You'll be far worse if you don't go away," she warned.

"My husband eats and he'll soon be home."

Suddenly the earth shook with the giant's footsteps. Jack ran into the house. "Quickly! Hide in here!" The giant's wife picked Jack up and slipped him into the  just as the giant came into the .

"Fee-fi-fo-fum, I smell the blood of an English-man," thundered the giant.

"You must be smelling the stew from last night," said his wife. "I'll bring you some."

"Never mind," said the giant. "Just bring me my magic hen."

Jack peeked out and watched the 🐔 lay one golden egg after another. Soon the giant was snoring.

Jack quietly grabbed the magic hen. But the hen cackled loudly and woke the sleeping giant. "Come back, thief!" cried the 👤 .

MY STICKER
WORDS
oven
kitchen
hen
giant

Jack ran like the wind. He climbed down the beanstalk but the giant was close behind him. "Mother, get an ax!" he shouted.

When Jack reached the bottom, he took the  and chopped down the beanstalk. Down tumbled the giant, and with a mighty groan he fell dead on the ground.

Jack and his mother lived happily ever after. Thanks to the golden , they never wanted for anything again.

MY STICKER WORDS
ax
eggs

LITTLE RED RIDING HOOD

Once upon a time, there lived a little  who was sweet and good. Her grandmother loved her so much that she made a [present] for the girl. It was a red velvet cape with a hood. The girl wore the [cape] every day, and so she was called Red Riding Hood.

MY STICKER
WORDS
girl
present
cape

One day, Red Riding Hood's mother said, "Your grandma is feeling sick, child. Take this  of bread and  to her. Remember, don't dawdle."

Red Riding Hood hurried across the meadow and through the forest. She had not gone far when out of the bushes stepped a big .

"Where are you off to on such a pretty day?" the wolf asked Red Riding Hood.

The girl didn't know what an evil beast he was, and so she answered sweetly, "I'm on my way to visit my grandma on the other side of the ."

"Wouldn't Grandma like some ?" the wolf said.

MY STICKER
WORDS
basket
cheese
wolf
forest
flowers

– 13 –

"I'll pick her some ," said Red Riding Hood.

While she wandered off the path, the wolf slipped away. He ran as fast as he could to Grandma's house and knocked on the .

"It is Red Riding Hood," the wicked wolf said in his sweetest voice.

"Come in, my dear," said Grandma.

MY STICKER WORDS
violets
door
spectacles
bed
ears

The wolf sprang into the room and locked Grandma

in the closet. Then he put on one of her nightgowns and

her  and jumped into bed.

Red Riding Hood came to Grandma's house and saw

the door open. She tiptoed inside and up to the

"Grandma, what big you have!" she whispered.

"The better to hear you with, my dear," said the sly wolf. "But come closer."

"Grandma, what big you have!"

"The better to see you with," shouted the wolf as he grabbed Red Riding Hood and locked her in the closet, too. Then the wolf ate the cheese and the bread and settled in for a nap.

A passing  heard the wolf's loud snores. He crept into the house.

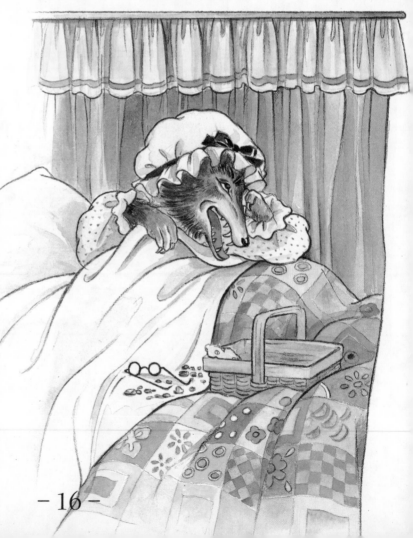

MY STICKER
WORDS
eyes
hunter
ax
Grandma

The hunter looked around and saw the locked closet door. He broke the lock with his heavy . Out popped Red Riding Hood and . The wolf heard the noise and woke up. When he saw the hunter and the big ax, he ran into the woods and was never heard from again.

Grandma and Red Riding Hood were safe and that was the end of the wicked wolf!

PUSS IN BOOTS

There once was a miller who had three sons. When he died, his sons split his property between them. The oldest son took the mill. The second son took the . The youngest son was left with the cat.

"My  can now earn a living. What can I do with a cat?" complained the youngest son. "I might as well make a fur out of it."

MY STICKER
WORDS
donkey
brothers
hat
cat
sack
boots
leaves

"Do not worry, Master," said the . "Get me a pair of boots and a sturdy . You will see that I am the best share of your father's estate."

Wearing his new , the cat hurried to a meadow where rabbits often came to eat. He put tasty  in the sack and lay down next to it, still as a stone. Soon a rabbit jumped into the sack.

Quickly, the cat pulled the drawstring tight and carried his sack to the king's palace.

"Here is a fine  for your table," said the cat to the king. "It is a gift from my master, the Marquis of Carabas."

Each week the cat caught another prize—sometimes a partridge, sometimes another rabbit. He gave them all to the king in the name of the Marquis of Carabas.

One sunny day the cat heard that the would be taking a ride by the riverside with his beautiful daughter.

"Bathe yourself in the today," he told his master, "and your future is made."

As the king passed by, the cat shouted, "Help! The Marquis of Carabas is drowning!" The king told his servants to help the Marquis.

"My master's have been stolen, my lord," said the cat.

"Fetch a new suit of clothes for the Marquis!" ordered the king. The miller's son looked very handsome in his elegant clothes. The  was charmed by him.

"Come ride with us in the royal coach, young man," insisted the king.

Meanwhile, the cat ran ahead.

He told the workers in the , "When the king asks

whose lands these are, tell him they belong to the Marquis

of Carabas." Then he ran on until he reached the castle of

a rich ogre. This  was the true owner of the sur-

rounding lands. The cat spoke politely to the ogre. "I have

heard that you can change yourself into an animal," he said.

"Of course," replied the ogre as he instantly became a roaring lion. The cat was terrified and ran up onto the roof. The changed back into the ogre. "That was frightening," said the cat, climbing down, "but I'll bet you can't become something small, like a mouse."

The ogre shrank into a . Quick as a wink, the crafty cat pounced. That was the end of the ogre.

The cat hurried outside just as the king's coach drove up to the castle. "Welcome to the home of the Marquis of Carabas!" he said, bowing low.

The king marveled at the  the Marquis. It was clear his daughter loved the young man. The couple were married that very same day. The cat became a great lord and never chased mice again— except for fun!

MY STICKER WORDS
lion
mouse
wealth

SLEEPING BEAUTY

Once upon a time, in a splendid castle, there lived a  and  . Their greatest hope was to have a child. After years of waiting, the queen had a beautiful daughter.

The king was so happy that he gave a big party to celebrate her birth. Among the guests were twelve good fairies.

The fairies gave magic spells to make the new princess beautiful, kind, good, and brave. Suddenly, a bad fairy burst into the castle.

"This is my gift to the baby," shrieked the bad fairy. "When she is fifteen, she will prick her  on a and die!" Everyone gasped in horror.

MY STICKER
WORDS
king
queen
finger
spinning wheel

"Do not fear," said the twelfth  who had not yet spoken. "I cannot undo the evil spell, but I can soften it." She waved her over the princess. "You will not die. Instead you will fall into a deep sleep and will not awaken for one hundred years."

To keep his daughter from harm, the king had all the spinning wheels in the land collected and burned.

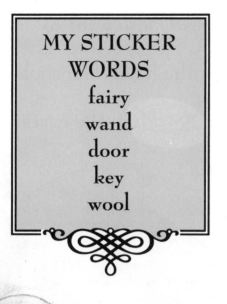

The princess grew in beauty and grace. On her fifteenth birthday, she went to a part of the castle where she'd never been. She came upon a small with a rusty in the lock. When she turned the key, the door sprang open. There sat an old woman spinning . The princess reached out to touch the spinning wheel, pricked her finger, and fell into a deep sleep.

At that moment, everyone in the castle also went to sleep. The king and queen fell asleep in the hall. The cook in the kitchen started to snore. Even a  in the eaves settled on its and went to sleep. Then a fairy placed the princess in her bedroom.

A great wall of rose briars grew around the castle. It was so thick and full of sharp that no man could get through it. For a long time, the story was told of the beautiful sleeping princess inside the castle. Many princes tried to cut through the with their swords but could not.

For a hundred years, everyone in the  slept. Then one day, another king's son heard the tale of the sleeping beauty. He rode to the thorny wall ready to chop through it with his . But for *this* prince, the rose briars parted and let him pass. As he searched the castle, all was quiet, touched by the hush of sleep.

When the prince found the

princess, she was so lovely that he bent

down and kissed her. Instantly, she awoke and smiled at him.

In every corner of the castle, dreamers awoke and rubbed the

sleep from their  . Hand in , the prince and

princess came to the great hall. They were married that

same day and lived happily ever after.

SNOW WHITE

Once upon a time, there was a king's daughter whose skin was as white as  and whose hair was as black as ebony. She was called Snow White. Her stepmother was a vain queen who was jealous of Snow White's beauty.

One day, the queen peered into her magic and asked, "Mirror, mirror on the wall, who is the fairest of us all?"

MY STICKER
WORDS
snow
mirror
forest
bears

The mirror answered, "Snow

White is fairest."

The angry queen ordered a

huntsman to take Snow White into the

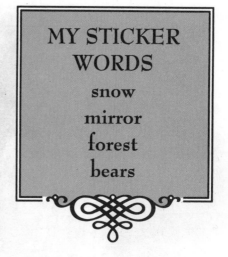 and kill her. The huntsman took

pity on the girl. "Go quickly. Run away!"

he told her.

As she ran through the forest,

branches tore at her clothes, and she was

frightened by and other wild beasts.

– 35 –

At last, Snow White came to a little cottage and went inside to rest. Everything in the house was small. There was a little 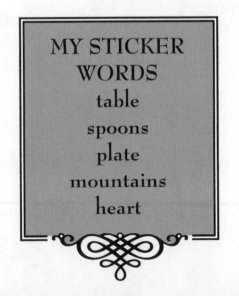 set with seven little plates and seven little ⬙. By the wall, there was a row of seven little beds. Snow White ate a little from each ◯ Then, she stretched out across the beds and fell asleep.

MY STICKER WORDS
table
spoons
plate
mountains
heart

When it was dark, the owners of the cottage returned. They were seven dwarfs who mined diamonds in the nearby  . The dwarfs were surprised to see Snow White, but they were friendly. When she told them about the evil queen, they asked Snow White to stay and live with them.

"Yes," she said, "with all my  ."

The queen learned from
her mirror that Snow White was
not dead but living with the dwarfs.
She was furious.

"I will have to kill her myself,"
she said. She disguised herself as a peddler woman. Into
her , she put a bright red, poisoned . Then,
she made her way to the cottage of the seven dwarfs.

"Delicious red apples for sale!" cried the  . The forest animals chattered loudly. They knew the apple was poisoned. But Snow White could not resist the shiny red apple that the peddler woman offered. With the first bite, she fell down as if dead.

The evil queen cackled with glee. "Now I am the fairest in the land!"

MY STICKER
WORDS
tears
box
root
eyes
castle

The dwarfs wept bitter  when they came home and found Snow White. They wanted to give her the best resting place. So they made a glass  and laid her in it.

One day, a prince was riding through the forest. He saw the beautiful girl lying beneath the glass. He begged the dwarfs to let him take Snow White to his kingdom, for he could not live without seeing her every day.

As his servants were carrying the glass box, they stumbled over a tree . The piece of poisoned apple fell out of Snow White's mouth. She opened her  and lifted the lid of the box. "Where am I?" she asked.

The prince was overjoyed to see her alive. "You are safe with me," he said. "Come with me to my  and be my wife." Snow White agreed, and they lived happily ever after.

THE THREE LITTLE PIGS

Once upon a time there were three little pigs. They lived with their mother in a cozy 🐷 sty. One day mother pig said to the little pigs, "It is time for you to go seek your fortunes."

The first little pig set out at once. On his way he met a man with a 🛒 full of straw.

MY STICKER
WORDS
pig
wagon
straw
door

"Please, sir, give me some

so that I may build my

house," said the first little pig.

The man gave him an armful

of straw and, before long, the pig had

built his new home of it. He was just

settling down to relax when there was a loud

knock at the . It was a big wolf!

"Little pig, little pig, let me come in," he said.

"No, not by the hair of my chinny chin chin," cried the first little pig. "I'll not let you in!"

"Then I'll huff and I'll puff and I'll blow your house in," said the wolf. He huffed and he puffed and blew the straw  down. The first little pig ran away.

The second little pig met a man with a load of sticks. "Please, sir, give me some  so I can build my house."

MY STICKER
WORDS
house
sticks
chin
chest

The man agreed and the second little pig built his house of sticks. He had just started to make his lunch when along came the wolf, hungrier than ever.

"Little pig, little pig, let me come in."

"No, not by the hair of my chinny chin 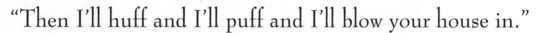."

"Then I'll huff and I'll puff and I'll blow your house in."

The wolf took a deep breath. His  swelled up.

MY STICKER
WORDS
balloon
wheelbarrow
bricks
letter
wolf

It looked like a [balloon] . He huffed

and he puffed. He puffed and he

huffed. At last, he blew the house down.

The second little pig ran away.

The third little pig met a man with

a [wheelbarrow] full of bricks. "Please, sir,

give me some bricks so I may build my house."

The man agreed and the third little pig

built a sturdy house of [bricks] .

Just as the pig sat down to write a  to his mother, along came the hungry wolf.

"Little pig, little pig, let me come in," said the wolf.

"No, not by the hair of my chinny chin chin."

"Then I'll huff and I'll puff and I'll blow your house in!"

The  took a deep, deep breath. He puffed and he huffed, and he huffed and he puffed until his face was purple. But he could not blow away the sturdy house of bricks.

The wolf was angry. He climbed on the of the house and tried to squeeze down the chimney.

The little pig quickly made a blazing fire in the . He hung a big pot of water over it to boil.

Just as the wolf came down the , the little pig took off the lid. Into the fell the wolf and that was the end of him. The little pig and his two brothers lived happily ever after in his house of bricks.

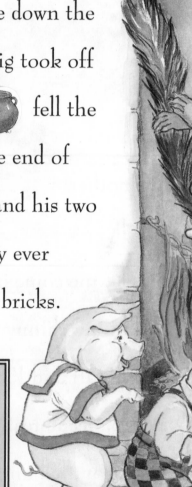

MY STICKER WORDS
roof
fireplace
chimney
pot

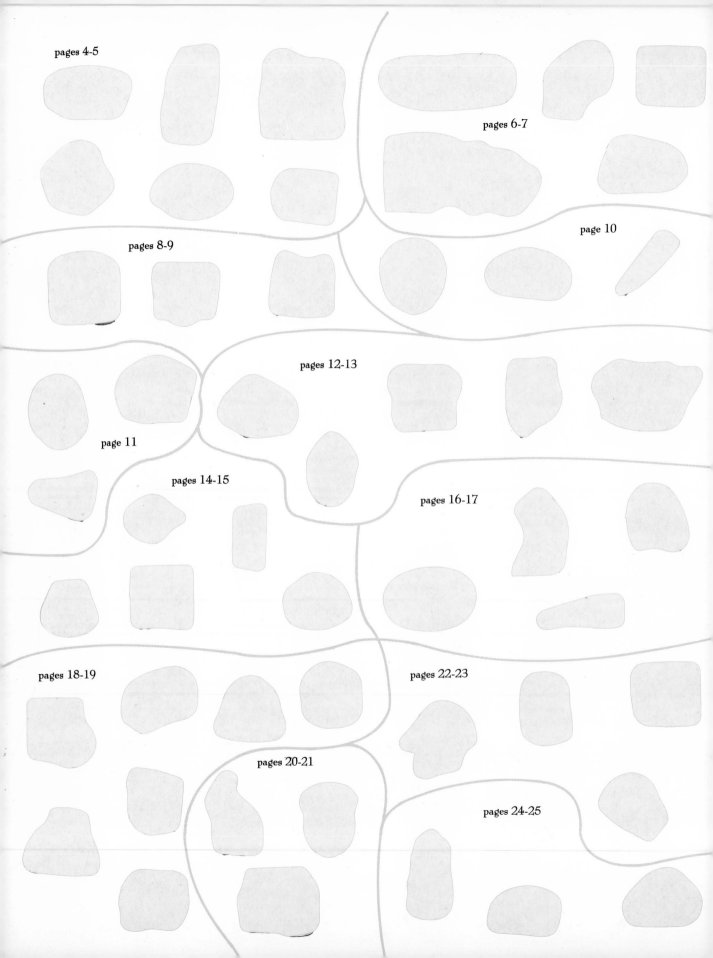

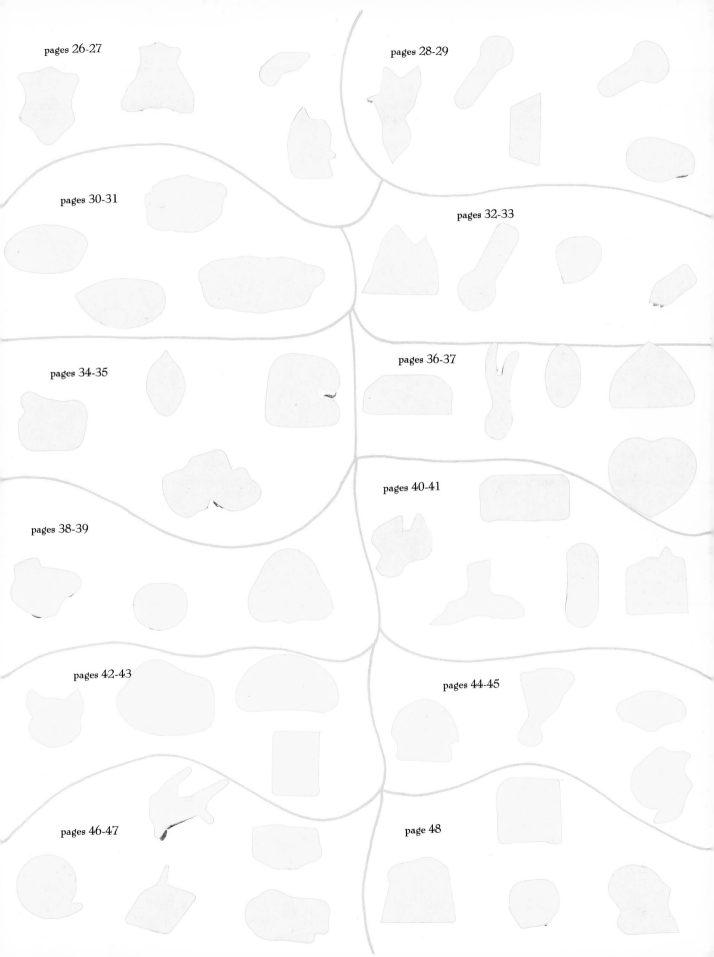

pages 26-27

pages 28-29

pages 30-31

pages 32-33

pages 34-35

pages 36-37

pages 40-41

pages 38-39

pages 42-43

pages 44-45

pages 46-47

page 48